Extinct!

by F. R. Robinson
illustrated by Allan Cormack

Scott Foresman

Editorial Offices: Glenview, Illinois • New York, New York
Sales Offices: Reading, Massachusetts • Duluth, Georgia
Glenview, Illinois • Carrollton, Texas • Menlo Park, California

Dinosaurs lived long ago. There are no dinosaurs now. They are extinct. That means they are no longer around.

Then how do we know they ever existed? People have found their bones!

In 1822, Mary Ann Mantell found
a huge tooth. She showed it to Mr.
Mantell. He saved things like that.

Mr. Mantell looked at the tooth. He said that it probably came from a huge animal. This animal was unlike any kind of animal alive then, or now.

After that, other huge bones were discovered. It was clear that these bones all belonged to the same group of animals. An expert named the animals "dinosaurs."

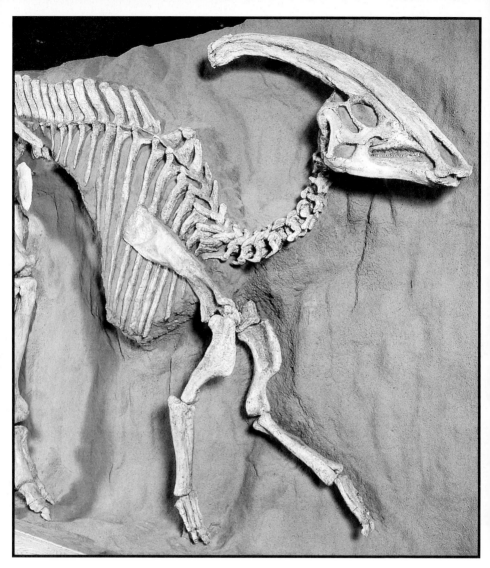

Since then people have uncovered
many dinosaur bones. About six new
kinds of dinosaurs are discovered
every year!

Experts look for dinosaur bones where wind or water has worn away the land. In these places, they can see layers of the Earth from long, long ago.

Experts uncover bones by
removing the rock above them.
Or, they remove the whole
chunk of rock with the bones.

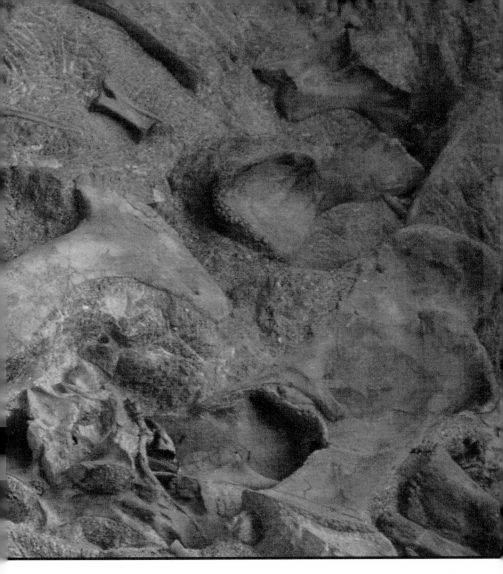

They wrap up the bones and rock.
They don't want anything to break!
Then the bones are shipped along to
a lab.

There, experts unpack and clean each bone. Then they rebuild the dinosaur. They try to put each bone in the right place.

Sometimes, bones are missing. Experts make fake bones with plaster or plastic to fill in the spaces.

Soon the dinosaur is put together. Then it is put on display for people to see.

What have we learned from dinosaur bones? Almost everything we know about dinosaurs!

Some dinosaurs were huge. Others were small. Some walked on four legs. Some walked on two legs, with their front legs up off the ground.

Some dinosaurs ate meat.
Others ate plants. Experts can tell
what dinosaurs ate by looking at
their teeth.

We know that dinosaurs hatched
from eggs. Sometimes a baby
dinosaur is found along with its egg.

Why did the dinosaurs disappear?
Dinosaur bones can't explain that.
Experts disagree about what caused
the dinosaurs to die.

But they do agree that it was a
good thing someone discovered that
first tooth! We have learned many
things about these exciting animals!
Who knows what we'll find out next!